WHERE AM I?

Written by Lisa Trumbauer

Illustrated by Judith Love

Harcourt Achieve

Rigby • Saxon • Steck-Vaughn

www.HarcourtAchieve.com
1.800.531.5015

S0-AXI-791

Where am I?

I can see the rides.

I can hear the music.

4

I can smell the popcorn.

I can taste the apple pie.

I can touch the goats.

I am at the fair!

How do you know?
Your senses tell you so!

Close
AND
Turn

What do you taste?

What do you touch?

What do you smell?

What do you hear?

We use our senses in many ways.
What do you see?

Your Senses Tell You So!

Written by Lisa Trumbauer

Harcourt Achieve
Rigby • Saxon • Steck-Vaughn

www.HarcourtAchieve.com
1.800.531.5015